FRESHWATER
FISHING BASS, TROUT, WALLEYE, CATFISH, AND MORE

Tom Carpenter

Lerner Publications Company • Minneapolis

Lerner Publications Company
A division of Lerner Publishing Group, Inc.
241 First Avenue North
Minneapolis, MN 55401 U.S.A.

Website address: www.lernerbooks.com

Content Consultant: James G. Dickson, PhD, wildlife biologist, researcher, author, professor, and hunter

Library of Congress Cataloging-in-Publication Data
Carpenter, Tom, 1962-
        Freshwater fishing / by Tom Carpenter.
            p.   cm. — (Great outdoors sports zone)
        Includes index.
        ISBN 978–1–4677–0219–5 (lib. bdg. : alk. paper)
            1. Fishing—Juvenile literature. 2. Freshwater fishes—Juvenile literature. I. Title.
    SH441.C357 2013
    639.2—dc23   2011050535

Manufactured in the United States of America
1—CG—7/15/12

TABLE OF CONTENTS

CHAPTER ONE

FRESHWATER FISHING FOR FUN

How many reasons can you think of to go fishing? There's fun—nothing beats pulling in a fighting, tugging fish. There's food—fried or grilled fish tastes great, if you keep your catch. And there's fresh air—being outside is always a blast.

Most people have freshwater nearby for fishing. Freshwater includes lakes, ponds, rivers, creeks, and canals. Freshwater is not salty as the ocean is.

Where to Fish

A lot of fishing happens on lakes. Some people fish in lakes as big as Lake Michigan or Lake Superior. But most lakes are smaller. Some lakes are natural. Many years ago, slow-moving ice masses called glaciers made many of these. Other lakes are man-made. One way to make a lake is to build a dam across a creek or a river. The water backs up behind the dam and forms a lake. Both natural and man-made lakes have good fishing.

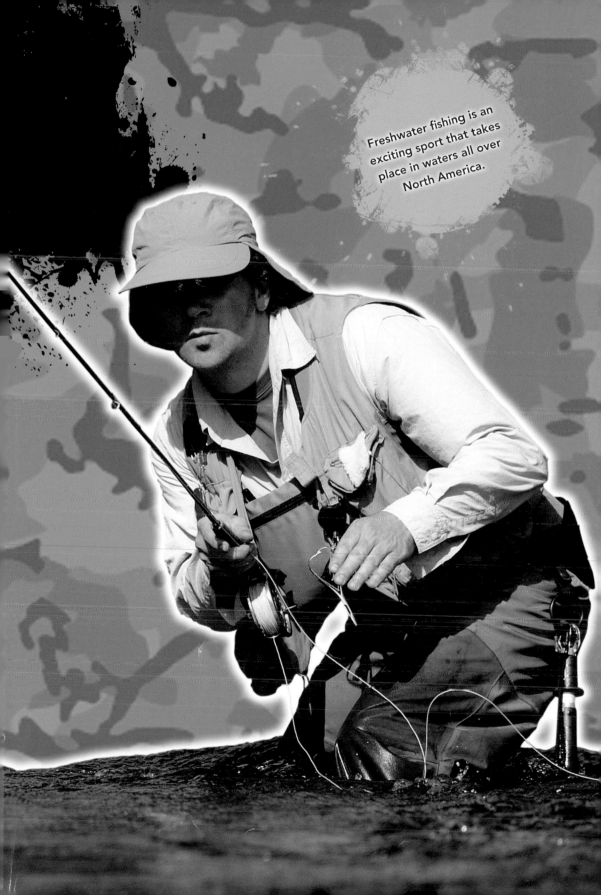

Freshwater fishing is an exciting sport that takes place in waters all over North America.

Rivers are exciting and challenging places to fish because the water is always moving.

Small lakes are called ponds. They are great for fishing because fish have only so many places they can hide.

Rivers are fun—as well as challenging—to fish in. The water in a river moves, sometimes quite fast. Fishers (also called anglers) have to know where fish go to get out of the fast current while staying close to their food. Creeks are smaller than rivers and for that reason are good places for beginning anglers. Sometimes fishers can wade right into a creek and fish.

In many places, canals offer good fishing. These waterways were created when people carved out a straight water channel and let river water flow into it.

Food and Fun

Fish that anglers catch for sport are known as game fish. Many fishers like to keep, clean, and eat their catch. Catfish and panfish are often kept to eat. Other anglers go fishing for the action and the challenge, and they release their catch. Releasing is letting a fish go so it can live and fight again with another fisher. Bass and trout are often released.

Sport anglers fish for fun. Popular species (kinds) of freshwater game fish include bass, sunfish, crappies, bluegill, catfish, walleye, pike, and trout.

In some large rivers and lakes, commercial fishing crews net or trap fish. These people fish for a living. They sell the fish they catch to grocery stores or restaurants. They are often after a type of fish called a buffalo or carp.

Bass put up a good fight when a fisher reels them in. This makes them fun to catch!

CHAPTER TWO

FRESHWATER FISHING IN THE PAST

Native Americans were the first anglers in North America. They created their fishing gear out of what was available in nature.

Because they fished for food, Native Americans often used nets to catch fish. This helped the fishers scoop up lots of fish at once. Strands for nets were often made of animal hair twisted together.

Native Americans also made wooden traps—cages with one open end. The fish could swim in but couldn't get out. Another effective way to fish was to stand in the water or on a rock ledge and spear or harpoon fish as they swam past. Spear and harpoon tips were often made of bone. Some Native Americans shot fish with arrows from their bows.

Fishing with a hook and a line was also an important technique. Native Americans carved hooks from bone, wood, or animal horns or antlers. Some Native Americans even used hawk claws or eagle beaks as hooks!

Many Native Americans relied on catching fish to feed their families. They made spears from the things they found in nature.

Fishing lines were woven from animal hair or from the long, thin plant threads found in cattail, hemp, and other plant stalks. Worms, grubs, caterpillars, grasshoppers, crickets, or pieces of meat served as bait. Native Americans tied bird feathers to hooks to attract, or lure, the attention of fish. This fake bait became the first artificial lures.

Angling Settlers

When Europeans started coming to North America in the 1500s and the 1600s, they brought their own fishing gear and techniques. They started developing fishing reels—spools around which fishing line is wound. Silk served as material for fishing line. Bamboo rods—long, thin poles—were also in play. But most early settlers weren't fishing for fun. Like the Native Americans, they needed to eat, so they netted fish too.

Settlers needed fish to eat, so they fished year-round.

These anglers became better at fishing. Fleets of boats brought fishing crews with nets to freshwater. These huge catches helped to feed people throughout North America. But all this fishing was slowly creating a problem. People were catching and taking freshwater fish faster than the fish could breed and replace themselves. Plus, settlers built houses and towns and grew crops across the land. Many waters became polluted. This caused fish populations to drop even more. Something had to be done.

Many early anglers used nets to try to catch as many fish as they could at one time.

CHAPTER THREE

FISHING RESPONSIBLY

Fish and game management was part of the answer. These days, each U.S. state and Canadian province has fish and game agencies. These agencies manage fish populations so that everyone can enjoy fishing. They set rules to encourage conservation—the efficient and careful use of natural resources. All anglers need to follow the rules. The future of fish and fishing depends on it.

Fish can't survive in polluted water. So without clean lakes, rivers, streams, and ponds, we wouldn't have fish. Stopping pollution of all kinds is also important in keeping fish populations healthy. Pollution can come from factories and farms, as well as from people throwing their trash into the water. Fish depend on all of us to protect the environment and keep waters clean.

Even pollution on land can damage fish and their waters.

NO DUMPING DRAINS TO RIVER

It is up to you to protect fish habitats so that future anglers can keep catching.

Adults need a license to fish legally. If an adult is caught fishing without a license, he or she may have to pay a fine!

Fishing Licenses

Adults have to buy a state fishing license to fish legally. Kids usually don't. Money from licenses supports fish and game programs.

Open and Closed Seasons

Fishing can only happen during open season. In some states, the fishing opener is a big event! Closed seasons protect fish when they are too easy to catch, such as when they are spawning (laying eggs to hatch new fish).

Size Limits

Some species can be kept only when the fish is over a certain length. Fish shorter than the size limit must be returned to the water. This rule protects young fish so they can grow up.

Some fish species are protected by slot limits. This means a fish that is within a certain length range must be released, but any fish longer or shorter can be kept.

Bag Limits

Bag limits make sure each person keeps only his or her share of fish for the day. But if you release what you fish, you can catch as many fish as you want!

Special Rules

Many lakes and streams have their own special rules. Two neighboring lakes may have different rules. Be sure to check posters and signs where you fish.

KEEPER
WALLEYE
MUST BE
18 INCHES
RETURN ALL OTHERS

BLUEGILL
CREEL LIMIT
10 FISH DAILY
MINIMUM LENGTH
8 INCHES

The maximum fish an angler is allowed to keep is also known as a creel limit. Fishing rules vary from lake to lake, so it's important to read all signs in an area.

GEARING UP

Like most fun activities, fishing takes some work to pull together. You need to find a place to fish, know what fishing gear and bait to get, and plan for safety.

A Place to Fish

Most fish and game agencies offer online resources where you can explore fishing spots. You don't need a boat for good fishing, especially on rivers and ponds. Creeks are just about perfect for fishing from the bank. Some lakes have fishing piers and rocky shorelines that work well too. If your family or someone you know has a boat, your choices of where to fish increase.

Fishing Gear

Some professional anglers own enough fishing gear to fill a store. But you don't need that much stuff to catch fish. Here are the basics when you're packing your gear.

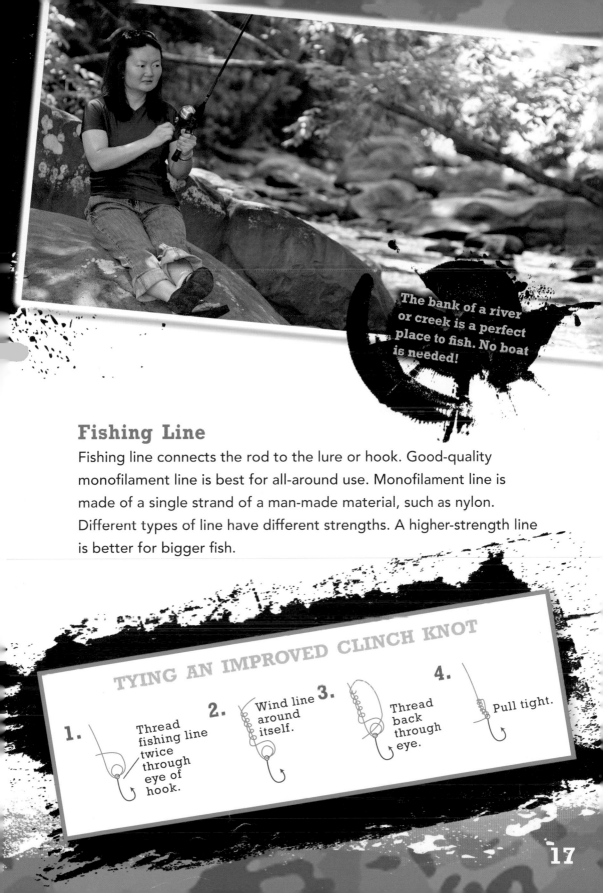

The bank of a river or creek is a perfect place to fish. No boat is needed!

Fishing Line

Fishing line connects the rod to the lure or hook. Good-quality monofilament line is best for all-around use. Monofilament line is made of a single strand of a man-made material, such as nylon. Different types of line have different strengths. A higher-strength line is better for bigger fish.

TYING AN IMPROVED CLINCH KNOT

1. Thread fishing line twice through eye of hook.

2. Wind line around itself.

3. Thread back through eye.

4. Pull tight.

Spin casting reel

Rods and Reels

Reels hold your line and help you cast your bait. A spin casting reel has a closed face and sits above the rod. An angler releases the line by pushing a button. A spinning reel is open-faced and hangs below the rod. A fisher releases the line with his or her finger. Rods are important for casting and fighting fish. Fiberglass is a common rod material, but graphite is better.

Fishing Bait

Fish often can't resist live bait, such as worms, night crawlers, minnows, leeches, and grubs. Live bait has the look and odor

Spinning reel

that attract fish. Choose bait for the fish you are pursuing. For instance, small minnows are perfect for crappies, while big minnows catch pike. On the other hand, a lively worm or night crawler will catch almost anything that swims.

Bait is easy to come by. You can even dig up your own worms for fishing.

Artificial lures work well too. There are many different types of lures that look like fish food. Some of the most popular kinds of fake bait are very lifelike plastic copies of live food such as minnows, crayfish, or worms.

Hooks and Sinkers

Most artificial lures have their own hooks attached. If you're using live bait or soft plastics, you will need to put it on a separate hook. Hooks come in different sizes, indicated by different numbers. The bigger the number, the smaller the hook. The bigger the fish you're after, the bigger the hook you need.

Sinkers take your bait down in the water to the fish. Sinkers were once made of lead. These days, it is important to use sinkers of other material. Studies showed that ducks, geese, and other waterbirds were getting lead poisoning when they swallowed lost lead sinkers.

Bobbers or Floats

A bobber or a float holds your bait at a certain depth in the water where you are fishing. When a fish bites, the bobber jiggles or goes underwater. Most floats are made of foam or plastic. Fixed bobbers attach to your line with a clip. Slip floats can be adjusted up and down the line for fishing at different depths.

Other Accessories

A landing net helps you land, or bring in, a big fish. A tackle box or bag holds your gear. Pliers and a knife help you change your hook and lure combination. And a cooler with ice holds any fish you plan to keep and eat.

A landing net will keep the big one from getting away!

A tackle box will help hold your gear.

Fishing Safety

Safety is important when fishing. Even if you can swim, you should always wear a life jacket when fishing. If you do fall in, your head will be above water, even if you hit it on something or faint from the cold water.

Always watch the weather. If a storm is coming, quit fishing and get to a safe place! Catching a few more fish isn't worth risking your life because of lightning or a tornado.

Consider the safety of others when you are fishing. Always look behind before casting. You don't want to hook a friend or a parent. That's one catch you can do without!

Even if you are a good swimmer, it is important to wear a life jacket when fishing.

CHAPTER FIVE

GOING FISHING

It's time to go fishing! But first, you need to understand the best fishing times and a few fishing techniques. You'll also need to learn how to care for your catch.

Best Fishing Times

Fishing can be good any time of day. Fish come into shallow water when the light is low. So mornings and evenings are great times to fish. Another good time to fish is on a cloudy day. Clouds may mean rain is coming, and fish feed as the weather shifts. But beware—rain usually isn't fun to fish in.

Fishing Techniques

The most common way to fish is to still-fish. This means you let out your bait, and it usually sits below a bobber. You wait for a fish to come past, take the bait, and pull the bobber under. This is a good technique for panfish and sometimes for bass and pike.

Anglers still-fish year-round. They drill holes in the ice to fish in the winter.

Another way to still-fish is to forget about the bobber and let your bait sit on the bottom of the lake or stream. This works well for catfish.

Casting is another technique. Cast out your bait and reel it back in. Most anglers use artificial lures for this type of fishing. Fish attack your bait as if it were fish food suddenly appearing. They get hooked trying to get away. Casting works for most game fish, such as bass, walleye, and pike.

In boats, trolling is a good technique that works to catch most fish. Let out your bait behind the boat, then row or slowly motor along, pulling the bait. You can cover a lot of water this way!

With jigging, you let out your line below the boat and then jiggle your bait to attract fish. Jigging works for most kinds of fish.

A jig lure is often used for jigging.

Setting the Hook

When you get a bite, you must set the hook. This means to firmly get the hook caught in the fish's mouth. Don't just start reeling, or you'll pull the bait out of the fish's mouth.

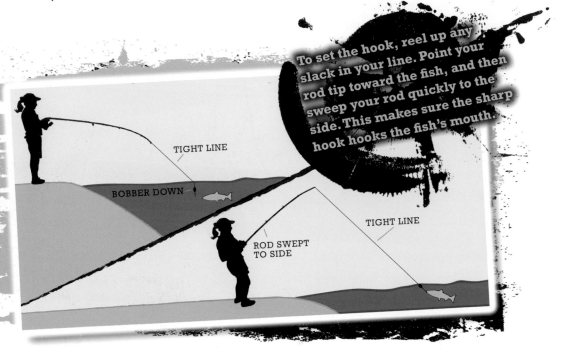

To set the hook, reel up any slack in your line. Point your rod tip toward the fish, and then sweep your rod quickly to the side. This makes sure the sharp hook hooks the fish's mouth.

TIGHT LINE

BOBBER DOWN

ROD SWEPT TO SIDE

TIGHT LINE

Fighting and Netting Fish

Fighting fish is fun. They tug, circle, pull, thrash, and jump! Keep your rod tip fairly high, keep reeling, and don't let your line go slack, or the hook will fall out.

To net a fish with a landing net, always lead the fish into the net headfirst. It helps to have someone else do the netting. You can also grab a fish by the lips to land it. But before you touch a fish, look out for any sharp teeth or fins that could hurt you. Don't touch a fish's delicate gills.

Caring for Your Catch

If you want to save some fish to eat, you need to take good care of them and keep them fresh. Put the fish you want to keep on ice in a cooler. Do not leave dead fish floating on a string or in a fish basket. They'll just stink!

Here's how to release a fish so it can live to fight again:

- Play, or reel in, the fish quickly so it doesn't get overtired.
- Wet your hands before handling a fish. Dry hands remove a fish's protective slime coating.
- Check for any teeth or fins on the fish that could hurt you.
- Remove the hook quickly.
- If the hook is deep, just cut your line. The fish's digestive juices will dissolve the hook.
- Slide or slip the fish gently into the water. Do not toss it.
- To help a tired fish, hold it in the water by its tail and gently move it forward and backward.
- Watch it swim away!

When releasing your catch, it's important to be as gentle as possible.

FRESHWATER GAME FISH GUIDE

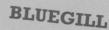

BLUEGILL

Bluegills prefer shallow, weedy water. A 1-pound (0.5-kg) bluegill is a big one. Bluegills fight hard and taste great. Still-fishing below a bobber is a good technique to catch bluegills.

CRAPPIE

Crappies like shallow water around stumps, brush, weeds, or other cover, but they like open water in summer. A 2-pound (0.9-kg) is a big crappie. Still-fish with a bobber, but keep your bait moving very slowly.

YELLOW PERCH

Yellow perch are easy to spot and catch. In spring look in shallow water around rocks or new weeds. In summer, perch go into deeper water. A 1-pound (0.5-kg) perch is a good size, but they can grow to 2 or 3 pounds (0.9 or 1.3 kg). Still-fish or jig for perch.

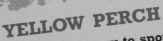

LARGEMOUTH BASS

Largemouths like warm, shallow, stumpy, weedy water with lots of cover. A 3-pound (1.3-kg) bass is a good size, but bass grow to 5 pounds (2.2 kg) or even 10 pounds (4.5 kg). Cast soft plastics or lures. Still-fishing with big minnows works.

SMALLMOUTH BASS

Smallmouth bass prefer cool water that has lots of boulders and rocks. A 2-pound (0.9-kg) bass is great, but they can grow to 5 pounds (2 kg) or more. Smallmouth are the hardest fighters of all! Use crayfish or minnows for bait around rocks, or cast or troll a crankbait that looks like a crayfish.

CHANNEL CATFISH

Channel catfish have whiskers that help them smell and taste food. Catfish live in rivers, ponds, and lakes. To catch catfish, still-fish with night crawlers or minnows. A 7-pound (3.1-kg) channel catfish is great, but they can grow as big as 58 pounds (26.3 kg).

NORTHERN PIKE

Northern pike are hunters with razor-sharp teeth. Never stick your hand or finger in a pike's mouth! Pike eat other fish, so they live where smaller fish do, usually in weed beds. A good-sized pike is 3 pounds (1.3 kg), but they can weigh more than 20 pounds (9 kg). Big minnows make good bait for still-fishing. Or cast a lure.

WALLEYE

Walleyes go deep during the day. But in the evening and at night, they come in toward shore or up on rocky or weedy areas. Troll live bait or a lure very slowly. An average walleye weighs 2 pounds (0.9 kg).

RAINBOW TROUT

Rainbow trout live in cold, clean water. An 8-pound (3.6-kg) rainbow trout is a great catch, but they can grow to weigh more than 40 pounds (18.1 kg). Cast into the water, and let the flow carry your bait to the trout.

27

HOW TO PREPARE YOUR FISH

Filleting your catch means to remove the skin and cut off the fish's meat. This gets rid of most of the bones. You can also scale a fish and remove its head and guts. Then you pick out the bones after you cook the fish. Ask for an adult's help to use a long, thin-bladed knife and to cook your fish.

How to Clean and Fillet a Fish

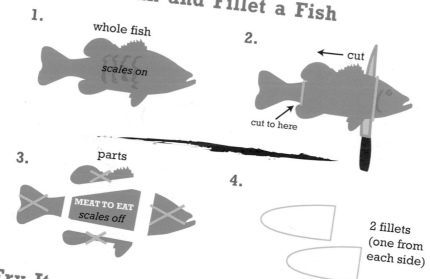

1. whole fish
scales on

2. cut
cut to here

3. parts
MEAT TO EAT
scales off

4. 2 fillets
(one from
each side)

Fry It

Heat a half inch (1 centimeter) of oil in a skillet. Roll fish pieces in flour or cornmeal seasoned with salt, pepper, and garlic powder. Fry fish until outsides are crispy and golden brown, about three to four minutes per side.

Grill It

Brush fillets with melted butter and a little oil. Then grill over medium heat for three to four minutes per side. Squeeze lemon juice over fish with a minute to go.

Bake It

Brush fillets with melted butter and a little oil. Place a fillet or two, plus two cut up carrots and one cut-up potato, on a piece of aluminum foil. Sprinkle salt and pepper on it all. Then wrap the foil into a package. Place in a 350°F (175°C) oven, on a grill on low heat, or in coals for an hour. A complete meal!

Taco-ize It

Cut up fish into small pieces, fry them, and use them as the meat in tacos with shredded lettuce, fresh salsa, guacamole, and shredded cheese.

Freshwater fish tastes great in tacos.

GLOSSARY

ARTIFICIAL LURES

fishing bait made from plastic, rubber, wood, or other materials to look like real fish food

CONSERVATION

the thoughtful, efficient, and careful use of natural resources

CRANKBAIT

a hard lure, usually shaped like fish food, that moves in the water when reeled in

GAME FISH

the kind of fish that sport anglers pursue most

LIVE BAIT

living fish food, such as worms and minnows

MONOFILAMENT

a kind of line, often used for fishing, made from a single strand of man-made fiber

PANFISH

small fish, such as sunfish and crappies, that are good for eating but not sold at a grocery store or a restaurant

STILL-FISH

to fish with bait that sits still, often below a bobber

TEST

the strength of fishing line, measured in pounds

TROLL

to fish by pulling live or artificial bait very slowly behind a boat

LERNER 𝒆 SOURCE™

Expand learning beyond the printed book. Download free, complementary educational resources for this book from our website, www.lernersource.com.

Further Reading

Befus, Tyler. *A Kid's Guide to Flyfishing: It's More Than Catching Fish.* Boulder, CO: Johnson Books, 2007.

Ross, Nick. *Fishing.* New York: Powerkids Press, 2010.

Seeberg, Tim. *Freshwater Fishing.* Chanhassen, MN: Child's World, 2004.

Websites

Fish Kids

http://www.epa.gov/waterscience/fish/kids/

This website from the Environmental Protection Agency has games and stories designed to teach kids about which fish are safe to eat.

Take Me Fishing

http://www.takemefishing.org/fishing/family/little-lunkers-learning-center

This website features fishing tips and information, online games, a hall of fame, and helpful fishing links and resources.

Young Angler: A Beginners Guide to Fishing

http://www.nebworks.com/kids/kids.html

Get fishing tips, including what bait to use, where to fish, and how to tie knots. This site includes a weather quiz to help teach you to keep your eye on the sky.

INDEX

About the Author

Tom Carpenter has hunted and fished across North America for almost five decades, pursuing big game, waterfowl, upland birds, wild turkeys, small game, and fish of all kinds. He has raised three sons as sportsmen and written countless articles and contributed to dozens of books on hunting, fishing, nature, and the outdoors.